THE ACCIDENTALIST

THE ACCIDENTALIST

THE 2012 DOROTHY BRUNSMAN POETRY PRIZE

W. Vandoren Wheeler

BEAR STAR PRESS

COHASSET, CALIFORNIA

THE ACCIDENTALIST © 2012 by W. VANDOREN WHEELER

All rights reserved.
Printed in the United States of America on acid-free paper
and distributed by the press & SPD (*www.spdbooks.org*).
Under the provisions of Fair Use, parts of this book
may be excerpted without charge for educational purposes
and in articles and reviews.

10 9 8 7 6 5 4 3 2 1

Orders & Inquiries:
BEAR STAR PRESS
185 Hollow Oak Drive
Cohasset, CA 95973
www.bearstarpress.com

Cover image modification: W. Vandoren Wheeler
Original photograph: Arthur Chapple, ca. 1910-1915, from the
    George Grantham Bain Collection (Library of Congress)
Photos of pilot Glenn L. Martin and a Barnhart biplane: courtesy of
    Alan Renga, the San Diego Air and Space Museum
Author photo: Sylvia Ciborowski
Book design: Beth Spencer

The publisher would like to thank Dorothy Brunsman
for her support of the press from its inception.

ISBN: 978-0-9850584-3-2

Library of Congress Control Number: 2012906439

ACKNOWLEDGMENTS

ANDREVIEW.COM: "Shopping Alone at Night"

Cider Press: "The Accidentalist"

Forklift, Ohio: A Journal of Poetry, Cooking, and Light Industrial Safety: "Slideshow," "Hinges"

George Washington Review: "Every Man Clearly," "The Spilling Out" (published as "Immaculate Pain")

H_ngm_n: "Pin," "A Warning to Nature Lovers"

Isotope: "And The Miracles Have Not Stopped Materializing"

Spork Press: "Dead Lab," "Official Apology," "Coat of Paint," "Your Favorite ____ Ever"

TABLE OF CONTENTS

I. ACCIDENT

CAUSE AND EFFECT	15
THE SPILLING OUT	16
GIVING BLOOD	18
DEAD LAB	20
DEAD LAB, DAY 2	22
AND THE MIRACLES HAVE NOT STOPPED MATERIALIZING	23
THE ACCIDENTALIST	25

II. ODD GOD

I SPOT A HOTTIE IN A CATHOLIC CHURCH	31
WHY SAINTS KNIT HAIR-SHIRTS	33
FIRST COMMUNION	34
EVERY MAN CLEARLY	35
COLORS OF THE CORRESPONDING JEWELS	37
WEDDING MUSIC	38
BOTCHED BAPTISM	39

III. ACCI-DENTED

YOUR FAVORITE _____ EVER	43
HOW WE SAY THINGS	44
NAMES	46
PET NAMES	47
APOLOGY FOR HOW APOLOGIES FAIL US	48
SLIDE SHOW	49
HINGES	50

IV. KITCHENING

HOME REPAIR ADVICE	53
I SIMPLY CANNOT OPEN THIS, THE WRAPPING IS DIVINE	55

KITCHENING	57
IN KITCHEN I FIND MYSELF	58
SHOPPING ALONE AT NIGHT, THE ARTIST GLANCES UP	60

V. CRUDELY DRAWN

ROAD TRIP	65
DEBT	66
A WARNING TO NATURE LOVERS	67
PIN	68
OGLING	69
PORNOGRAPHY	70
NUDE BEAUTY	71
OF THE OWLS, PUPPIES, AND SHEEP, I WAS A SHEEP	73
AFTERNOON I FELT BIPOLAR	75
DRAWING	76
PICTURED ANIMALS	77

VI. ODD BLOOD

CIRCUS ACT	81
PRODIGAL SON	82
COAT OF PAINT	84
I PAINT SELF-PORTRAITS OF HORSES	86
REAL TEETH	88
PASTORAL MEDITATION	89
SCRAP PAPER	91
NOTES AND THANKS	95
ABOUT THE AUTHOR	97

8:23 And he took the blind man by the hand, and led him out of the town; and when he had spit on his eyes, and put his hands upon him, he asked him if he saw ought.

8:24 And he looked up, and said, I see men as trees, walking.

8:25 After that he put his hands again upon his eyes, and made him look up: and he was restored, and saw every man clearly.

—The Gospel of Mark

I
ACCIDENT

CAUSE AND EFFECT

The lights rise just before the film finishes.
The pinball machine blacks out before swallowing the last ball.
I load the shotgun to end our rabid dog,
but he's already splayed in the yard.
As I reach for the bus cord, the sign illuminates with a *bing*.
I call to leave a message and she answers.
At the airport I shake hands with my father and see
his shoulders awkward with the hug he'd have given me.
I twist the bulb to change it, it lights up my hand.

THE SPILLING OUT

This artery of cars I'm in
skims past its vein, each cell we are
slightly meandering: only a broken
white line between
hundreds of possible head-ons.

I would pull over, disappear
by lying down in that flowered
field—if not for its hidden bees.

The fear of pain is the leash
with which the body
minds its wandering.

From the parking lot I can smell
the dentist's office—a drill squeals *ríí*
in each door's hinge. I resist writhing
on the waiting room chair as the dark
worms of cavities eat into my teeth.

I so hate and need cleaning.
I am acutely alive, so
often complaining.

What do I know of pain?
A bus's accidental handrail
and crude back operations
cast Frida Kahlo in
a wretched corrective posture.
She painted her veins open.

I'm relatively safe in my envelope
of coagulating blood, which protects
well enough against syringes

and the mis-tugged
tartar hook that would otherwise
start the spilling out
that will leave me, eventually, to myself.

My immaculate teeth and I take a wrong
turn on the way back from the bathroom,
and see a hole in a Mexican man's gums
I could put my pinkie through.

My unease swerves into his—
BAM! I am so grateful,
I might as well have seen an angel!

GIVING BLOOD

My superstitious nurse friend
swipes a cotton ball cooled by alcohol
across my forearm, readies
the cylopic syringe.

I wince, and she says, to distract,
that she once worked on a boy
with skin so pale, every wandering
vein in his face was traceable, says
it looked like a net of blue
threads pulled his skull back.
She doesn't laugh when I—funny
me—ask, *Think he's a Pisces?*

That woman in last night's restaurant:
something I don't pretend to understand
had pruned her torso of its limbs.
She waited in a tall wheelchair studded
with padded braces that held
her tilted head upright. Her waiting seemed
so intense . . . her glance clipped my gaze
into a stunted smile I swallowed awkwardly.

That man with a stub hand
in my ballroom dance class, and
my ridiculously happy sister, who can't
do simple math or read but loves
in a purity that shames me:
they just made it to this
side of the threshold
before the door closed on them—

the sight of my blood, mute
in a tube, reduces me to a lanky

child in a butcher shop,
seeing for the first time
separated, all the parts
that make up a life: muscles,
ribs, entrails, that vulgar
red over everything.

I vaguely hug my friend goodbye,
run my empty finger over
the flesh of her shoulder,
tracing what is held together
by countless seams.

DEAD LAB

They look so real, I think, these bodies
drained of goop and dried for students
to pull apart like leather clocks.

Skin peeled away and pinned
open, our insides are sculpture.
It's the stubble that troubles me.

Scrubbed up and blue-gloved,
I can't resist the urge to hold my palms
before me like surgeons I've seen on TV.
I flinch when the door slams shut
from the air pressure used
to ventilate the room. I spot

on the table a head
sawed so clean the
eyeball still
rests in its socket
like a tiny, plastic
Easter egg, emptied.

Each is, or was, elderly: the body's
return—ashes to ashes and such—.
arrested chemically.
They don't look like dust.

The lab tech says to treat them
as if they were alive. *This lady's
bones are so thin, you'll break
both femurs if you yank.*

The saw offers us a side-view:
coccyx tucked in, tucked

like a tail—curled like a finger relaxing . . .

my grandmother's, after she nudged
a playing card my way,
all the red diamonds
aligned with her hand.

DEAD LAB, DAY 2

As if peeling old fruit,
I pull the sheet from her face—
uneven teeth, eyes
closed, an earlobe
and its tiny hole

stretched open by years
of an earring's half ounce.
Up close, it resembles a mouth.

Such a relief she's a stranger!
Why was I so scared
I might know her?

AND THE MIRACLES HAVE NOT STOPPED MATERIALIZING

In grade school, Ben Chavaría made me press
two stones together, hard, until finally
I magnetized them! And the miracles
have not stopped materializing.
I learned my body
brims with antibodies!
Migrant birds repeat their routes
using earth's magnetic currents
as a map. Some poor penguin taught us this
when we discovered ferrous oxide in its head.
Penguins! Our doctors grow us

new appendages: attach the suggestion
of ear-shaped, polymer frames, then
plant a cell like a seed . . . at least our bodies
know what to make of it. Or reconstruct
ribs for a kid whose heartbeat
visibly shuddered his chest,

knowing he could grow up
to die as old as anyone, just as sad.

Our hearts are awkward clocks.
If we didn't slow them down
with exercise, or speed them up
with trans-fat, every sixty thumps
would mark a minute.

Our decisions unsettle time.

Online, I try to convince my friend
about the ghost in his machine.
He has a problem with the word *ghost*.

The other problem: he's a computer, programmed
to beat me at chess. We have our differences.

Indonesia's president might've started a civil war
while his country still sleeps. Some might wake
with a farming tool in their neck
around the time I'm going to bed. Which
is worse, that I know this and brush my teeth,
or vice versa? Indonesians have no problem
with the word *ghost*. It is a version
of stardom: their dead are pictures they pray to.

At that, my friend laughs as best he can
and takes my bishop with a pawn.
I could reprogram him into agreeing with me,
but the sentences would be equations
that only equal themselves:

Me in my Body = the Arc in its Ball

Look at that: a tour bus of retirees
wide-eyed as infants, thanks
to penultimate heart attacks.

They snap pictures of their own gardens
on their way to the Grand Canyon
again. Soon they'll zoom past a baseball diamond,

behind it a cemetery. I can't stop imagining
the sound of leather-wrapped cork
knocking against those stones.

THE ACCIDENTALIST

When I finally took up my father's razor
to clean the hair from my head, the scar
I found resembled a seam, the kind
that hides a zipper. I tugged away,
ready at last to reveal the wonder-
ful World of Me: to stand in awe
above the plunging depths
of the infinite, interior universe, to touch
the bright source of this tenderness
I project from my sleepy eyes . . .

But my skull with its cover removed:
a poorly molded self-portrait
trapped in a cheap snow globe.
How pathetic, to be underwhelmed
by one's own imagination. I must
have been considerably depressed. I stood
plastically, like a bored action figure
ankle deep in fake flakes. I shook
my head in disappointment—
everything turned a jumbled white.

Three of us snuck behind the yellow bus,
squatted, huffed, and took turns standing up
to have the other two squash our chest
against the bus's tin siding, which buckled.
The sky, specked with white clouds
rushing from my eyes, subsided.
To paraphrase our parents, What the hell
were we thinking? Still, it was thrilling
to dangle our legs into this
unseen abyss that waits inside us.

Whatever had left, slowly seeped back in.

When it was Travis's turn, he fell
to his side and twitched, so we ran
for help, eventually. I thought of you, Father—

felt the fear that propped you up, pulled
you taut as a tent peg toward the sight
of two dogs crossing the field
to close their dog jaws
on my sluggish body.

The white door of the hospital opens
to the white of the hospital.
Later, I tripped over a particular rock
and opened my skull on another.
Without anesthesia or consent, J. yanked
my caveman's heart from its cave.
It stammered in the sunlight.

My existence is a sequence of accidents
for which no one offers insurance.
They told me the scans revealed nothing
out of the ordinary. They told me nothing
they could see was broken. They told me

for years, or, for years, they told me,
nights I wandered into the desert,
swallowing still-wriggling lizard tails,
sipping water from pinched cactus parts
squeezed between two flat rocks.

Once, I awoke, legs frozen in a puddle
of stars—that was my perception, due
to the cold. The stars were in the sky.

Still my hand reaches for that ice
ice-pick with which I chiseled

myself out, for the quickened
breath of grasping it, for the relief

of letting it go. Travis, by the way,
is fine. I only feel my feet
when they fall asleep,
and they take
forever to wake up.

II
ODD GOD

I SPOT A HOTTIE IN A CATHOLIC CHURCH

I wait for her
to kneel. Her silk
blouse yawns.
Yes.

An unexpected shaft
of sunlight shuts
my eyes, my skull
its own cathedral.

Its windows let yellow
light angle in. Dust floats
illuminated, monastic
motes who only break
their vows of silence
to rail against chastity.

Religious duty shaves
our curls off. We don
tiny hair shirts woven
by our gnat apprentices
(the goal is to grow
smaller—this is difficult,
but easier than endless
questioning, i.e. *Do I
want her form
of love more than God's?*).

I lose patience praying
for patience, ask
for a quick cancer to corral
our will into six weeks
of pure devotion. The lit
candles shake their heads

in golden disappointment.

Around us, stained-glass saints
suffer torments rendered
in colors of freshly cut fruit.
The light from their halos
keeps our eyes squinted closed.

My gaze averted
upward, I awkwardly lay
the cleavage after-image
upon the raw wood of a pew.

We must not look upon her,
so we look *not* upon her,
and whatever else we look upon
is not what we see.

This is why we embroidered
on the inside of each habit's hood:

VISION IS REVISION—
KEEP IT HOLY
HOLY HOLY!

WHY SAINTS KNIT HAIR-SHIRTS

> *When we take a very cold shower, we feel very alive.*
> *It is difficult to take a cold shower. It is difficult to*
> *remain very alive.*
> —the shrinking genitals

Twenty pesos bought me a towel
and a used soap cake. Three minutes running,
the water was still smack-gasp

cold and the world
condensed itself into the inches
between my pried-open eyes
and the wall's peeling
blue paint: cracked robin
egg blue, Caribbean ocean
postcard blue, rickety Mexican taxi
blue, a brand new—no, I saw it
from inside it. My shiver wasn't
mine, but a salamander vertebra
vibrating through me. A set
of larger lungs shoved
into my chest panted
in bucket upon bucket
of, sí, evanescent air.

My clacking teeth clipped
that moment into bits
I swallowed. It is in me.

Now I light like incense
this sense intensification
to let it coil up out my mouth,
and defy the gravity of even
the densest of sentences: there
I was, now make me more this.

FIRST COMMUNION

She said my name and the curtains behind me
caught fire. Incense spiced my sinuses
as her lust dilated me like an antihistamine—
it particled my brain celestially.
Behind the crosses of scaffolding,
saints gawked at angels painted
naked on the ceiling, who welcomed us
with open arms into the kingdom.

Perhaps I owe it to the wine we'd pinched.
Perhaps. But that won't unrosepetal
her lips from mine—my mouth opened,
as if for the first time, to the taste
of someone else's salt. One sip
of her tannic saliva plastered me
against the surface of my formerly abstract
craving made concrete as the floor we pressed
each other against, so desperate not
to disconnect anything touching.

She snuck out first. My blood
spilled inside me, from a cup
overturned. I could look up at Him,
hanging in an infinite desire, and mourn
as one man mourns for another.

EVERY MAN CLEARLY

Lyric	Action
I may never march in the infantry,	[stomp in place]
Ride in the cavalry,	[hold imaginary reins]
SHOOT! the artillery,	[clap, make a cannonball fist]
I may never fly over the enemy,	[arms as wings]
But I'm in the Lord's Army, YES SIR!	[stiff-backed salute]

God was the imperceptible sphere formed
by innumerable spy satellites capable
of determining whether or not
my dinner fork lay right of my salad fork.
By the light of His infrared gaze I tried
to count how many sins I could scrape
out from under my fingernails, lost
track, grew sleepy, woke up in the infantry
of the Lord's Army. Those pushups
they made us do only made my arms
tired and when I asked if the enemy
was also doing pushups and if
so, how many could they do,
and who won the Last Great
Pushup Battle? When I asked
that they made me do extra.
My fellow GI assigned to clean the latrines
helped me perfect my insubordination:
appreciate that hiss of a lit
match dropped into the toilet!
Let's call God
unjust—He'll just fry us
with His holy magnifying glass
and remain in the right, since
it's His magnifying glass, His light!
I learned to use cleaning supplies

to graffiti bright heresies
into the grime on the ceiling.
At my court martial, the corporal-slash-attorney
accused me of striking doubt
against flint to light faith's
tattered curtains (I wanted
to let more light in).
The courtroom door shook
with a gentle knocking.
My Lord, Your Honor, I see
men as trees, walking
into a forest of fire that does not consume.
I appealed my case
to a higher court, where I was found
guilty and my sentence
was perpetual forgiveness.

COLORS OF THE CORRESPONDING JEWELS

Jesus visits me as a giant
bald eagle might.

His golden talons clasp my shoulders.
He lifts me high above the neighbors,

above poverty, above the flashing gaming palaces.
I whisper to myself the good deeds He's seen me do,
imagine the colors of their corresponding jewels.

Then He lowers His curved beak, brushes
my earlobe, You let me lift you up like this,
yet blush at the sound of my name.

From that height the city seems a puzzle
poised to fall apart. The horizon, a fading
halo, and in the toy trees

crows in black frocks hunch over
seeds they gnaw upon, then
drop to the miniature street.

WEDDING MUSIC

This worship song
has me singing I am,
or will be, Christ's
bride. The next note
trembles my throat,
my slender body.

The veil catches
in the brambles
of my beard. Tears

smear eyeliner
down my cheeks,
blackening my teeth,

the spittle my laughter
flings into the very air

He lifts me into
by my cleansed armpits.

His presence
obliterates my dress.

My weird god
straddles me—

music isn't
imaginary
anymore:

I am hymn.

BOTCHED BAPTISM

Pardon the God-
                slobber—he's had me
in his vast mouth.

Human hands held my head
and shoulder blades, served
the purpose of His teeth.

Forgive me, but crows filled
a nearby tree like a squawky choir.

                I brought a very bleached towel.

I said to hell with ritual:
                I want the metaphor
                  made physical. Therefore,
I slipped my wide-eyed minister
a twenty to hold me
under till I went limp. He didn't.

Still, they said my eyes
were brighter after.

How am I supposed
                to tell you this?
I practiced dying
to get better at living?
It felt like a theatrical miracle.

                When little, trying to cross
                the pool without surfacing,
                I tried to breathe just a bit
                of water sucked in
                through clenched teeth.
                I thought it worked.

I only pretended
to plug my nose: river amoebas
made a universe of my body.

The very cold re-
                minded me
I was an element.
                        Did I wear the appropriate T-shirt?
                        Should it have been black, or white?

The cold I hoped would kill
the old me made my heart
                        thick in my constricted chest,
                        lungs ushering all
the more air in.
My limbs trembled
like a puppet
                skeleton.
                        My skeleton jaw
rattled on its hinges.

I saw Jesus standing
in a painting before
a shut door, his gentle,
lifted fist . . .

Knock, knock.
Who's there?
Want to die to myself.
Want to die to myself who?

Wait, I messed up.
                Let me try this again . . .

III
ACCI-
DENTED

YOUR FAVORITE _____ EVER

Please participate.
I've made an engine of
my apoplexy, and I have
no idea what that means!
It just occurred to me/us.

It likely means I suffer
from a pathological
need to sound
interesting.
I want this to be
your favorite thing.

Watch me toss this
verb into the air!
It will never come back down.

What an embarrassing beginning . . .

Let's reset by saying *mumbleberry
mumbleberry*. I am imagining
your lips moving.

Let's instead imagine a horse,
a plain brown one, galloping
along its fence next
to the highway.

Roll the window down.
What, as we fly by,
should we shout out
into the wind roaring in?

HOW WE SAY THINGS

I can't get over how we say things,
like it's a hill I've decided to ski up.
My friend on the phone: *Cancer took
my grandmother*, as if she'd been repossessed
by the IRS. When my own died, I was asked,
How are you holding up?, as though I were
a miracle of architecture. My unmusical brother
notes my tendency *to fall in love*—
shouldn't that mean it's harder to climb out of it?
And yet it's the same in Spanish, *caer enamorado*.
I read what a Spaniard said about the sensation
of a kiss, that each time it's to stand at the edge
of an abyss. I have always had that feeling,
but never knew until I read it. Words dictate us
like a loose science, sensations sketched out
in delicious, irresolvable equations.
When I was little, an Indian on television
(feathers in his hair, even!) said, after a fellow
Indian's demise, *Words are heavy, like stones. Birds
do not speak. They only sing, and fly.* As we soared
two feet above a set of equidistant steel rails,
the Brit standing in the aisle hissed
down to his wife (who refused to look up)
*You never say what you think, rather
what you think you meant to say*, then
excused himself to the water closet.
I find such pleasure in telling you
that the passengers *fell silent*.
What altitudes we've risen to,
not knowing how or when.
Words are bird bones, my brother:
hollow, to allow for flight.
Break them open
in your teeth, add them

to *a hearty stew*,
or put them in birds.
Why, here come a few
Pacific Swallows, as if called
by the jaws formed
by that dead tree and its shadow.
Dare I say the little things are *alighting*?

NAMES

Fly works. Butterfly doesn't.

Starfish don't look
like stars or fish.

Koalas are distinctly
un-bearish.

Pencil lead is, of course, graphite.
Tin foil? Aluminum.

Hammer on a fingernail
to know its weakness.
Puffer fish—too obvious.

Spaniards calling urchins
sea hedgehogs seems
clever, but then your sense
sense asks, Where is the hog?

They should be called unihorns.

I don't feel lied to.

Let's just work on a word
for an unseen leaf
that becomes a grasshopper

buzzing an arc
that remains in the air
even after
it's gone again.

PET NAMES

I can't call you Honey
without making me
a cartoon bear,
or mindless bee.

I am not hip hop
enough for Baby.
Sugar, cheap.
Dear has me as
some buck in heat.

Ah, a hidden
explosive, or an endless
tunnel I am lost
inside. I call you Mine.

APOLOGY FOR HOW APOLOGIES FAIL US

At least an infant's coffin
is easier to lower
into the ground.

It only takes two people.

Wait, come back.
It isn't a coffin.
It's a box of oranges.

I can't give you an orange.

Okay, it is, actually, an infant's
coffin—but there isn't
an infant inside. The child
is safe, somewhere.

I can't tell you where
the child is safe, but what
a relief it isn't here!

Right? Here, take this
strange orange.

SLIDE SHOW

I have nothing insightful
to say about memory.
I could describe a random moment
I remember, include a pair
of details sharp as thumbtacks
to hold up the white sheet
of some vague emotion
upon which you would project,
with that soft light
from behind your eyes,
a moment you had half
forgotten, which would give you
the feeling that we share not
that memory but
something large enough
to contain them both, and even though
the curl of this someone's particular
smile would evoke a subtle blush,
as though you had been caught partially
undressed in a public place,
it would feel in that instant more yours
than anything else, anything
I could ever offer you.

HINGES

Will it ever seem helpful, in any way useful,
that when you remember looking from your moonlit
backyard into your nearly dead, elderly
neighbor's window in hopes of resting,
for a time, your incessant gaze upon the elegant,
despondent silhouette of the grandfather clock
standing guard against her wall, but
instead catch the image of her hunched shoulders
shrugging off that faded, duck-print dress—
what purpose does it serve that when
you recall this moment years later
in a nearby, nearly empty bar, you can't
help but see yourself as a boy digging in a back-
yard, searching the dirt for the metal toy
you hid from your older brother—a tiny
truck, lemon-rind yellow, with a delicate,
chrome-like door handle so
well rendered you once pinched at it
with your fingernails, thinking hidden
hinges might let it swing open?

IV
KITCHENING

HOME REPAIR ADVICE

Keep in mind that *The Glass
Menagerie* is a melodramatic play.
When driving a nail, hold it with a pair
of needle-nosed pliers you don't care for.
Buy expensive tools. This makes a difference.
Don't club a porcupine because it is eating
your aspen trees. Wait for a better reason.
The handsome side of wood should be
what the saw's teeth enter first.
Don't stab your pregnant wife. Don't stab
your unpregnant wife. Don't stab your wife
in any way. When you paint, load the brush,
thick like peanut butter on good bread.
When you are standing on the banister above
a stairwell, and you think *I don't want to fall
now*, listen to yourself. You are correct. Just relax,
and don't think of falling. Think of standing.
When you need to destroy a significant
structure, invite your best friends
over to help. Paint therapeutic phrases
on the walls before you smash them.
Wear eyeglasses. Almost
always, except when making love.
This is when you should remove
also your eyes, your skin, and do
the work with those explosives packed
into the cracked center of your being.
By the way, make love only with your wife.
When digging a deep hole, imagine,
underground, the steel
shovel striking flint.
You alone can see the muted sparks.
Make a menagerie of the toy animals you find
in the yard, in the basement. Arrange them

upon the windowsill, with intention, around
improvised principles. But if they begin
to speak, question what they say. Compare it
to advice your grandparents gave you.
Reconstruction will always take
fifty percent longer than you think.
Carry various sizes of screws around.
Hate, hate, hate, hate mold.
Kill it with light or bleach.
When you are making a point
by raising your voice, do not let
even thunder upstage you.
However, smashing your glass on the floor
does not make an exclamation mark.
No matter what you have said,
when you are finished
speaking, lean forward.

I SIMPLY CANNOT OPEN THIS, THE WRAPPING IS DIVINE

I get drunk and think I always have been.
The shapes people make move past
like overweight, tropical fish,
fanning out expensive fabrics, dangling
the luminescent lures of diamonds
before gaping mouths. The fanciest
cradle their cocktail glasses
like gigantic jewels, and with the other hand
gesticulate as if tying the air into sailing knots.
My eyes won't stop oscillating between
the surfaces of textile and skin:
a publisher's mohair jacket sleeve
drawn across her silk-less thigh,
a waiter's polyester pants brush
the wobbly attorney's ring finger—
so many sensations in these intentional
and accidental touches . . .
But everyone's waiting for someone
else to arrive. No one is comfortable
when anyone's glass is empty.
As new wine is poured, one must pinch
the stem and swirl. Full-bodied,
yet discreet as good help.
A curly-haired woman in a tight dress
slinks past the table of exquisitely wrapped
gifts no one in here wrapped
and I'm tangled
in the tendrils of her hair.
It feels like she walked off with my belt.
I would toast desire, but I don't want
to embarrass the host. I too would sneak
upstairs and listen in on the affair disheveling
the freshly disinfected bathroom,

but I'm occupied by this doctor
trying to talk a hottie into the unlabeled
regions of her body: It contains
such exotic locations . . . the Tunnels
of Guyon, the Canals of Schlem—here,
for instance, float your Islets of Langerhans . . .
Someone on the couch knows a new
grandma who was asked what she wanted
to be called. Some late cabernets can be
so fruit-forward. She said, in all earnestness,
Nobody ever called me Pretty. Some sentences
pour whatever's left in my glass onto the floor.
The homely Honduran maid, who often sneaks
shiny fashion magazines from the trash
to study our language's fickle spelling rules,
wipes up the mess before anyone notices.

KITCHENING

So content in Kitchen, you
convinced us we could not
leave the house for the right
ingredients, and so conceived
a lasagna we should have called
something else. Kitchen
had us pinching goofy samples

into each other's gaping mouths,
pancake mix instead of flour
added an oaty overtone—extra
mozzarella compensated, sorta,
for the lack of proper cream.

Kitchen inspired us to chop and open
soda cans into aluminum foil
for an oven cover, but first you
splooshed in more uncalled-for wine.

The meal itself: forgettable.

We found the most culinary
pleasure in making
out . . . Little we touched
and didn't taste.

We couldn't think of what
to call dessert. The fig sauce
Kitchen smeared across

your lips drew mine
into them again. I don't
know who is eating
whom. I can't
say I mind.

IN KITCHEN I FIND MYSELF

In Kitchen I find myself
confounded. The concept
of local groceries grown
by sort-of neighbors caresses me
into a dopey hopefulness.
What I buy waits
a few days then rots.
I compost half the apples
I arranged on my table
in a tasty Nativity scene.

I truly enter into Kitchen
only when with you,

but today I am sufficiently
enticed by scantily dressed lettuce . . .
Maybe caress some spinach—
blanched (look up blanched)—
with white wine cream something
something! A side of hollandaise
from backyard eggs
smeared over whatever . . .

Then, perhaps, a tenderly
slaughtered cut of meat, simmering
in its own juices, as the scent
of organic mushrooms
mushrooms in my mind!
Oregano, O! Fresh crème fraîche

spurts across butter and sugar
slathered over peach slices
set like lips

in the center of a white plate:
a perfect sculpture my hunger
arranges in the messy Kitchen
of my imagination . . .

SHOPPING ALONE AT NIGHT, THE ARTIST GLANCES UP

Oh, Moon, I am lonely. Nope.
Alone, I am moonly: effaced,
distant, melodramatic. Yup.

My wan expression floats
over the earth and its distractions.
My sadness emits a soft glow
grocery-goers note and ignore
to be polite. They remember
how it was—no point smearing
their glossy pity over me.

Before the baby, the successful
wedding ceremony, this mother
now guiding her cart heavy
with the accoutrements of love,
(the "don't worry" of hot dogs,
the "you will almost always
be safe" of lentil soup)—
she thought she might die
in a room filled with cats.
In my version, it's books.

As I stand in the directionless light
of the check-out line, like a silhouette
of emotion, I become a beacon of darkness
reminding everyone to be grateful
for even their predictable relationships.

The cold from the frozen dinners
stacked in my hands seeps into
my finger bones, my wrists,
and yes, my despondent genitalia.

And I let it, since the pain is so
obviously symbolic, its meaning anyone
can grasp, since the symbol's
creation is a transformation
of hurt into art,
and because it feels as cold

as outer space must, and there is
no one pressed by gravity to the face
of this wide planet who does not
either love or miss the sad,
cold, hopeless moon.

V
CRUDELY DRAWN

ROAD TRIP

When you finally pull over,
the road becomes oddly still.

Other cars move up and down the road.
They are what make it a road.

Traffic talks past the grass.
Sunlit insects.

A hand-painted sign says it is okay
to pick your own fruit. We don't.

We watch the horse rub against its fence.
We watch it as if it were something else.

DEBT

I can't afford any more lightning shows—
I am still making payments
on last summer's sunsets.
I must have a million invoices
stitched by industrious bees.

Why do these leaves insist
on glowing as if love were not
only possible, but visible—it is
disturbing. And how dare they turn
most vivid just before they die.

I refuse the fleeting
splendor of half-dead trees!

Yes, for Christ's sake, I resist
the forest's solace. My peace
awaits in the next world.

So I reject the suggestions
of cloud formations.
My imagination is helpless
as it is, besotted with all
this useless beauty.

Please stop
parting storm clouds
with casual gestures of sunlight.

Let me be.
I can never repay You
for what You have done to me.

A WARNING TO NATURE LOVERS

The mountain laments
that it can't taste
the climbers it eats.

Something clouds
resemble: white cancers
mushrooming through a blue brain.

Another thing rain
is like: tiny eyes opened
by the fall, terrified
by the razors of flower petals.

Bugs go airborne
to keep from being
eaten. Birds meet them
there, in the air.

At dusk the sky becomes a flesh
from which unseen claws
draw diminishing colors . . .

In a dark forest, the trees
surrounding us seem
infinite. Who can describe
these pine needles
as they rise toward us?
What are they
injecting us with?
Some illogical impulse
to cuddle bear cubs?

Oh, why not? Whether
we run or just
play dead, Mother
will maul us all.

PIN

My mind is an Omnimax.
The fly fishing instructor made me hold
a dollar between my elbow and my ribs.
Rainbow trout actually exist.
The photography instructor pins the prints together and squints.
The hole left makes the print a practice.
In the plastic carousel, stale vacations await.
Other carousels dizzy kids.
Satan sculpted all the sugar I ever ate into another me.
Closed my eyes to see him more clearly.
Fiskars makes my favorite scissors.
Everything I remember of Arizona fits in a Viewfinder.
I don't remember Dad being there. He was.
Our ice cream melted nearly instantly.
Red thumbtacks I experienced intensely.
My experience of a popsicle is really
your experience of another popsicle.
My college photographs became me.
Photoshop stopped my glossy heart.
There isn't anything like a stream.
The trick really is in the wrist.
Dad pulled the fishhook from my thumb.
My mind puts it back in.

OGLING

Breasts are best when
the subject is upright.
Like this they appear less
animal-like. Though I have
learned to love, finally,
the way they taper
when she bends over

to gather a splattered dessert.
You will disagree, but I think
of this as progress, thanks
to my imagining that all
the nerve endings, those slender
vases of spiraling glass,

drain, like a jar's last
drop of honey,
their sensation into
the over-flowing
thimble of her nipple,

which will not
in that moment pour
across the touch of anyone's
tongue, or into anything
at all, and so the potential
pleasure vaporizes, not
into nothingness, but
into the air around us.

PORNOGRAPHY

The magician taught us,
through repetition, the trick:
saw a lipsticked woman
wearing a sequined bikini

in two. Don't let
her screams sound
practiced. Dis-
play, then slap her

halves back together,
and she will leap
up out of the box
smiling, waving,

to absolve the nervous,
applauding audience.

Watch how that
hand blooms.

NUDE BEAUTY

Set down that over-poured glass
of cooking wine—you have ogled
the rain long enough, long enough
to hypnotize yourself
into nibbling these crackers
as communion wafers,
and the inaudible hymn this appetizer
inspires creates such a din
you can't hear the steady, blue vowels
flames recite underneath the pan.
With the scratches in its Teflon,
its surface seems crudely drawn.

Damn that synthetic coating,
and all surfaces, and the illusion
that wobbles your sight when
you look at the fine screen in a screen
door, and when you are hungry and want
nothing to eat and when you can't
draw, which, for you, is all the time.

The vision from the museum
of a naked woman illuminated
by thick light falling from heaven
has become a long *hallelujah* you can't unhear.
Her nudity magnifies the vulnerability
tiny in her eyes, which fills you up
with the urge to either cup her
every word in your palms like a hurt bird,
or hump her pale body into blushing.

Your mind tries to move her
arms over her naughty bits,
as in *The Birth of Venus*,

but the beams of light hold
her limbs fast. Take

a deep breath. Note that
rain coagulates on the concrete
like drops of clear olive oil.
Ah, olive oil.
Picasso was raised on it,
they put it in his bottle.
Ah, Picasso.

Your eyes will eat what they will.
Listen to the salted and peppered meat
sizzle in the pan, rasping,
I want you, I want you.
What is your name?

Molecule by molecule you become
whatever you place on your tongue.

OF THE OWLS, PUPPIES, AND SHEEP, I WAS A SHEEP

Many of us are arranged on a bus.
Girls swaying under headphones
wired to the same walkman
lip-sync each to each.

Inside every bad song is the lyric
I LOVE ME, but inside every decent
story is the lyric moment.

I figure three more stops until mine.
I figure when pop songs speak to you,
you know you're depressed. The verse
      She shakes her thing
      all around the room
is trying to say she jingles her keys
at my luggage locks, since I really do
lock my luggage, which hints at tender issues.

I need a deeper voice to sing
      You paint my grey sky
      blue blue blue!
It means it's just a big bowl turned blue
thanks to fake paint and we are bugs,
trapped, about to be fumigated,
but isn't our prison gorgeous?
The bowl's blue—it's complicated because . . .
who knows? We didn't come up with blue.

I was so proud of myself when I realized
      I feel like a cartoon brick wall
means his emptiness holds
the shape of her body as it left him.
Pain fashioned so beautifully.

But when I finally figured out it's not
hair lip, as in a-scar-thin-as-a-*hair*,
but *hare*, as in looks-like-a-rabbit,
I felt sick to my stomach.
Whenever we lined up
to sharpen pencils the Sheep
went last:
          run and you fall, stab yourself dead—
and we stumbled around the room mumbling,
pencil's lead gooping our blood
into a grey mud. But then I was told
it's not true, all those years it was graphite—
which can, incidentally, unstick locks—
and the worry seemed silly, for years,
until some five-year-old on the news
fell on her upright, freshly
sharpened pencil, its tip lodged
a half-inch into her heart.

She must have looked like a collage
as she walked up to her teacher,
who knew enough to not pull it out.

If I were that smart, I'd fill
this half-empty bus with a lament
about my own half-emptiness.
But the first note would break
my voice in two, so instead

I shove this pencil into my chest,
the wrong key stuck
in a lock rusted shut.

AFTERNOON I FELT BIPOLAR

Two paint tubes and the incalculable colors
in between—the right music turns off
whatever turns off everything:
birds simultaneously brushstrokes
and quarter-notes, my shirt sleeve solicits insects
from the grass, fingernails and violin strings
drawing reeds from the pond as the tremolo
of greens and reds convince trembling
flowers into opening petals opening petals!

Getting sloshed on color's nectar
is almost enough to distract the eye
from what waits behind: rocks like lumps
of tedious observation. Those weightless,
wandering mountains, more like black gases.
The fence smeared into the horse, poor
septaplegic fence-and-horse . . .

Now each object just utters a word
obviously misspelled, an unintelligible,
self-interrupting echo. Each image's
failure stands in as anti-matter,
obliterating presence in a half-instant.

But if the blue frogs in my head
die when I paint them, this means
they were alive, and intensely.

And if the mind is the eye's trumpet,
today I'm content to play out
in accidental syncopation the inebriated
melody of these reverberated,
crayon-scrawled, half-known notes.

DRAWING

The writer friend showed me a photo
of a sculpture of a vague face
carved from a single aspirin.

I wanted to squint at it
until my head hurt,
then swallow it.

Instead, I sketched
a freshly emptied water glass,
and smiled as the medicine
reminded me of medicinal feelings . . .

PICTURED ANIMALS

I must appreciate
most what isn't
cup: the space green
tea soon becomes.

The absence of
an ostrich fills
the living room
with anticipation.

That I am sitting
alone is thrilling!
I might dance monkey-like
on the coffee table, smoke
roomfuls of Moroccan tobacco.

I am grateful, too, you
are gone. My calm mind
can make you anyone
who's just stepped out
for a to-go mug of cocoa.

And yet the elephant
saucer we bought
with wedding money misses
the elephant cup you kept.

I didn't mean to hold
this meditation up—my eyes
stopped on the blank
of wall where the Chinese
scroll you brought back

isn't: two cranes,

which mate for life—one's
beak tip poised inside
the curve of the other's neck—
makes my fingertip twitch.

You are probably
riding toward me
on some magical animal
I haven't yet thought up . . .

Who would I become
should I smash this cup?

VI
ODD BLOOD

CIRCUS ACT

The craziest thing I did today was pick,
from the candy bowl at work, a ROOT BEER,
a ridiculous flavor, but it makes me think
of my father, the time I heard him say,
as if it were a confession, "I like the taste
of root beer," and it felt like a door
opened in what I always thought
was all wall, and it shut again
by the time our burgers came.

That circus just us boys watched
in a different city—I hated it,
Texas or somewhere, while Mom and Sis
wandered the mall. The elephants
were obviously sad. When the trapeze
ladies pushed through the thick
red curtain, bare arms raised in V's,
slinky in glittering rhinestone bikinis,
my father leaned over, whispered, "This
is my favorite part" and my child's heart
seized—it was the end of our family!

Would I choose home and Mom
and vacuum half-empty rooms,

or learn to juggle fire, throw
knives into the wooden
door some kindred
orphan girl was tied to?

PRODIGAL SON

One year I went as a whiny vampire.
I went as a cowboy, and the weight
of my cardboard horse rubbed
rope burns into my shoulders.
Before I was old enough to enjoy
the irony, I went as an M&M—
a piece of candy demanding
more pieces of candy.
I went as Judah, king of Israel,
and as I waited under
a papier-mâché crown, my mother
ran across our dark lawn
for some staff I would wield—
when her ankle tendon
snapped under a misstep,
I understood I was to fetch Dad,
and that, despite her state, I would
still be taken to the party,
where my eyes would radiate
under the eerie gym lights after
downing fistfuls of colored sugar.
I went as a loud-mouthed ninja.
I went as a silent astronaut, and Dad
made a helmet of a plastic fish bowl
duct-taped to my chest plate,
and released me into the night.

I went as my favorite version of myself,
diffused into my hippest T-shirt and jeans.
I went as a skinny alien, a thoroughly
lit Christmas tree. I went as Jasper
the Fucked-Up Ghost, I went
as a bottle of champagne,
and the champagne was my fermented blood.

I went as a drink spilled down
some drunk angel's blouse, as whatever
the hell they wanted me to be.

I came as one out of the desert,
haggard, bearded, mute
and stoned with thirst.
My father stepped back before
the arc of the old door pulled
open, and he, he knew me.

COAT OF PAINT

It's cold, and my plastic jacket's
zipper feels like stitches.
I never thought I'd survive
anywhere you spend most
months wrapped like food
you keep fridged.

I miss the pretty much
pure sunshine of the desert,
but not the heat headaches.

Before I left, an Albuquerque
girl I wanted bought a big ol'
car from some grandma.
What a great 8-track!
Of course it couldn't play
anything we liked:
We were learning how
to love what was old.

We painted its long doors
yellow, looped a purple
flower over its green hood.

I predicted the house
paint she picked wouldn't
stick. We didn't

make it. She drove
that boat past me
five years later, yellow
and purple as
a new bruise. Oops.

I have gotten used
to cold, but not rain.

Is that car gone?
When I see it again,
I will be dead.

I hope its door open.

I PAINT SELF-PORTRAITS OF HORSES

> *Animal glue is all around us, even in the binding of books ...*
> —Animals and Ethics pamphlet

The horse weighs down
the exhausted field.
Both their backs bow
under half the sky.
Old muscle, field of weeds
trodden and flat-teeth-clipped . . .

Around the field, a fence
of crumbling wood.
Around the horse legs, its tree-knot
knees, either flight paths
of flies, or motion lines
of a trembling: my twinging
at the stitches lashing
the pacemaker into
my grandfather's chest.

These flat, childish mountains,
obviously drawn in one motion.
Worst are the flowers, for those set
on their—on her—kitchen table.
She couldn't finish saying,
Those are so beaut—

              the pleasure and sadness
smashed together, shattering into something
she choked on, then swallowed.

This mesquite bush's tangle,
so two-dimensional. What I hoped
made a bird, shrivels into more weeds.

What I thought formed a simple shadow,
for some semblance of balance,
throws back its head, parts

crude teeth to bite,
and another form
of desperation paints
its skull see-through—
my brains split
like a horse's hoof.

God, grind this grief into
a glue that holds
these images in
their ink, patient
shapes to stain
my paper mind.

REAL TEETH

My God my life is empty
and dull, except when
dying, but I am always
dying, and so it is boring.

Mama Dot has been half-dead
for a decade. Will it hurt
to ask her why she's still alive?
She slumps in her mobile chair.
She looks like a moose
stupefied by an empty highway.

I would love to see her
angry. I can remember, barely,
who she was when Papa C. passed.
She reached for the vase, lost hold
of the face she was propping up—
fell into her true self and sobbed
into some chrysanthemums.
I hoped to someday hurt as much.

Now her favorite thing is steak.
You'd never know from the look
stuck to her face as she gums
what they've cut up.

Christ! Release some wild
animal to tear into my house
to eat my food, shred
my books, chase me from room
to room, breaking every plate
and picture frame until I turn
to rear up to meet it, all fear
and saliva and bared teeth.

PASTORAL MEDITATION

I rest my vision of the world
as a blank white page
upon my upturned palms.
I crumple it. This tide is out
to kill me. The waves would not hesitate
to beat the living snot out of my body,
and those sand crabs dream
of picking my frame clean. This sunset
best resembles a drop of blood pressed
onto the microscope slide in my mind.
If I touched it, my finger would fry—long
before I got that close, *I* would fry, run
out of oxygen, freeze in the depths
of space, all those stars staring past me.
To those attempting to become
One with the Universe: the White-Eyed
Assassin Bug sprays acid and stabs
with its proboscis. The protozoan *Plasmodium*
hates you with malaria, which weakens
your immunity to insanity. Once attached,
the Mexican Painted Gila Monster, though
beat dead, will neither unclamp its jaws from
nor stop injecting poison into your swollen forearm.
It waits in rock fissures. The fissures
continue on for miles, curving with the bluff,
their staccato points, tongs of a music box
pricked by sunset's light, hills beyond
base notes, blue waves pouring out dark
that pools in shadows between each rock
radiating music. Each note deepens a shadow.
Each shadow hides a Gila Monster.
His short, fat tail swings with each step
as you cradle his weight with your good arm,
the pebbly skin a texture

you will never forget
for as long as you live.
After an hour, the poison cocktails
your cerebral fluid and the sunlight
careens off his pink, marbled head,
off the multitudinous scales
in orange, yellow, and white
notes of the tune of a spinning
mobile dangling oh
such excruciatingly beautiful lizards,
whose jaws, when they finally unlock,
call up to you as they fall, Forgive me!
Forgive me for what I have made you,
a violent, suffering, quivering mass, forget
the cruel things I called you, the time
I didn't answer the phone when you knew
I was home, forgive me for failing to ever
become a loving father, for all this bitterness
I taste in your blood—
I promise, oh I promise
it will never happen again.

SCRAP PAPER

I wish this were written
on an old envelope.
Finally, I am sorry.
I hope you can still read it,
given the present . . . Never mind.
Once, I shot a dove. A grey dove, and it was
hunting season, but still, a *dove*.
Unless they take away my one wish,
I'll use it to blow that bird back up
into the sky, those tiny tufts
of down sucked up into its chest
as if by a hiccup, and it's a bird again, until
it dies again. Pardon my condition,
but I've been reminded my heart is nearly dust.
When they arrive to retrieve
the notebooks, the black box, whatever
in me records these proceedings,
I hope they don't close my eyes.
Or maybe I'll die old, and angels will pry
at the hinges of my ribs to open up
my chest like an old barn door.
Scrawny bats will fly out, a cat's
skeleton won't. No more paper. A storm
of electric messages will momentarily electrocute
those who truly loved me—tiny bolts
of lightning illuminate their misty eyes.
They will jockey for the most moving
summation of my pros and cons,
then ask what's to be done with my CDs.
Being of sound mind, etc., I am,
most likely, sorry
for what I have done,
and sorrier that it does not matter.
Let's hope *this* is the last form of spam

you ever get from me. I trust that, soon
after reading, you will hover above
some kind of treadmill to delay
your own heart's return to a cup
of ash. Sentences such as this one
make it tough to continue ruining
perfectly good pieces of paper
with sentences such as this one.
It could just continue on
forever in its white purity, ironically
resisting the reason for its creation
with articulate emptiness,
until some yokel burns with the need to make a grocery list.

        sliced turkey
        butter
        2%
        o.j. (pulp free)
        3 tomatoes (or 2 larger ones)
        carrots, carrots, oh carrots

NOTES AND THANKS

"Of the Owls, Puppies, and Sheep, I Was a Sheep" contains a line ("I feel like a cartoon brick wall") from the R.E.M. song "Why Not Smile?"

Thanks to Tom Sleigh, Roger Fanning, Dean Young, Marianne Boruch, Pete Turchi, Tony Hoagland, and Matthea Harvey. Marcia Southwick, thank you for pulling me out into the hall. Grrraawwrrr to Jay Ponteri, Scott Nadelson, Natalie Serber, Jesse Lichtenstein, and Erin Ergenbright. Thanks to Matt Hart's hair and lungs. Thanks to my wonderful family, and my understanding wife.

ABOUT THE AUTHOR

W. Vandoren Wheeler was born in Las Cruces, NM. He earned a dual English/Spanish degree from New Mexico State, University of New Mexico, and Universidad de Granada. Warren Wilson College granted him an MFA in Poetry. He teaches writing and literature in Portland, Oregon, where he lives with his wife.